GODDAMN ATTITUDE

GET BUSY LIVING OR GET BUSY DYING

BRADLEY CHARBONNEAU

REPOSSIBLE

Copyright © 2021 by Bradley Charbonneau

All rights reserved.

No part of this book may be reproduced in any form or by any electronic or mechanical means, including information storage and retrieval systems, without written permission from the author, except for the use of brief quotations in a book review.

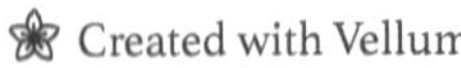 Created with Vellum

DEDICATION

To: *those who didn't get to meet my mom*

From: *those who did*

"If you knew who walked beside you at all times, on the path that you have chosen, you could never experience fear or doubt again."

— WAYNE DYER

PREFACE

"Of course I'm going to miss my mom. I'm going to miss our daily talks, my walks in the woods with Pepper, and I call my mom.

Why?

Because she lifts me up. She's my role model. I thought about it, 'How did she get there? How did that happen?' And then I think about the comments we're getting lately about my mom and saying, 'Oh no. **But I need Dede.** Dede lifts me up. I rely on her to show me the positive aspect of it. I need her. She helps me. She guides me. I don't know what I'm going to do without her.'

And that's when I think that there is going to be a vacuum that is left in this world when she passes and that we, our job then, is to fill it, and to rise up and to fill that void of positive, upbeat silver lining that Dede Charbonneau always sees.

Anyway, that's my goal."

— BRADLEY CHARBONNEAU, YOUTUBE RECORDING, JUNE 11, 2020

The above text is an excerpt from a video I recorded the day before mom passed away on June 12, 2020.

Sometime in the fall, a friend in my Toastmasters group here in Utrecht said that I needed to write a book about my mom.

You'd think that I, Mr. "Ooh, I had a fleeting thought! I should write a book about it!" that I would have thought about that.

But I hadn't.

It took:

1. Recording this video
2. A friend telling me I needed to write the book

for me to, the very next day after talking with him, go and put the title and cover (and empty book) up on pre-order for sale way into the future on June 12, 2021, on the one-year anniversary of her passing.

This book was *triggered* by that video and the outpouring of love I got on behalf of my mom from the people whose lives she touched.

You can see the 9-minute video here: ga.repossible.com.

Trigger.

I love the word. I hope this book triggers events for you, whether you can take Dede's stories and change your own life, improve the attitude of others, or even write your own book about your own mom (or dad or whoever influenced you) and share their stories with the world.

CONTENTS

Introduction   xi

Foreword   xv
By Leah Dines

1. Stories   1
2. Stop and Say Hello   3
3. Random Acts of Kindness   5
4. Write a Note to a Teacher Who Has Helped You in Some Way   9
5. Attitude. Are We Born With It or Can We Learn It?   12
6. The Little-Known Secret to Helping Yourself (and Improving Your Attitude)   15
7. Read to Your Kids   18
8. It's the Thought That Counts   20
9. Without You   23
10. Don't Be Too Sure   25
11. Fun, Quirky, Brilliant, and Unafraid   27
12. Fun Money   31
13. "I Hate Reading"   34
14. Most Of Us Had Never ______ Before   39
15. In My Heart She Lives Forever   42
16. Love is Not a Zero-Sum Equation   45
17. "We're terribly sorry, Ms. Mall, but ... "   48
18. A Looker   52
19. The Traveling $1,000+ French Haute Couture Dress   58
20. Roulette   60
21. Vignettes   70

Afterword   77
Acknowledgments   81
About the Author   83
Also by Bradley Charbonneau   85

INTRODUCTION

This is one of those "I can't not write this book" books.

I don't have a choice (OK, fine, I realize I have a book called Decide, with the subtitle, "There's usually a choice, it's usually yours.").

So I have a choice.

I *choose* to write this book.

Once I was *triggered* to the idea, I became *driven* to write it by a power greater than me.

Maybe I see my mom in a light that's brighter than others. Maybe I think she's greater than she really was. Maybe she was just an average mom and one might wonder if a book needs to be written about each and every mom.

In fact, now that I write it out like that, I **do** think it would be a good idea for each child to write a book about his or her mom.

Hmm, maybe this will start a trend.

Was my mom special? A superstar? Extraordinary?

Well, frankly, yes.

But that's not why I'm writing this book.

I'm writing this book because of examples like this from my mother's life that impacted those around her and my wish, my dream,

my mission and purpose is to strive towards having even a fraction of
the impact she did on people in a positive way—and sharing that
with as many people as I can.

Take this quote from the chapter titled, "Stop and Say Hello."

"How I wish I had known at the time what an impact a simple act of
kindness could have on someone's day and life."

— Dede Charbonneau

Mark Twain has a quote that is appropriate here:

"If you tell the truth, you don't have to remember anything."

— Mark Twain

If we realized "what an impact a simple act of kindness could
have on someone's day and life" then I'm fairly certain we would act
accordingly.

I like to think we would be more giving, loving, and fun. But hey,
maybe there are some out there whose idea is to make other people's
lives miserable. This book is not about those types of people but they
are more than welcome to read this book.

What if we acted every single day as if we were impacting the lives
of those around us?

Do you believe it's possible that simple acts influence others?

What if they do?

Might we act differently?

If one tiny little thing, one little story about my mom changes the
tiniest little element of your life for the better than this book has
served its purpose and my mother's legacy lives on through you to
reach another person you will reach.

Do we have a deal?

You learn one little thing in here and pass that on to someone
else?

You might be thinking, "Gee, this Bradley Charbonneau writer dude thinks that tiny little acts from individuals can change the world for the better."

And if you thought that?

You'd be exactly right.

Welcome to *Goddamn Attitude*.

Repossible

P.S. I have a series of books under the "Repossible" name. In each of those books, I end each chapter with three bullet points:

- Possible
- Impossible
- Repossible

Here's an example of how I might use or "define" each one:

- **Possible:** tomorrow
- **Impossible:** yesterday
- **Repossible:** today

Or:

- **Possible:** good, "this could work"
- **Impossible:** difficult, "yeah, well, but why?"
- **Repossible:** optimal, "Oh yeah. Here we go."

It "forces" me to then summarize each chapter as best I can using these three variants. As I have been working on this book, I realized I missed these elements at the end of each chapter so now I have added them. I hope they add something for you, too.

FOREWORD

BY LEAH DINES

MOM

Who do you call when something exciting happens...or something that scares you to the core.....I called my mom. Maybe you do too. Maybe you call your best friend. She turned out to be both for me.

But the really interesting thing that I didn't expect happened in the past 5 years. When I wanted to say something that wasn't really appropriate, or probably shouldn't be said about something or someone at all, I started calling or texting my MOM! We had so many laughs at things that I never thought I would share with MY MOM!

Yes, she was there for all of the serious stuff about life, raising twin daughters, work, and responsibilities in general, but to get to know your mom as a true friend and share the fun sometimes weird or wild things was really fun, and sometimes eye opening.

She was a good listener and could always find the bright side or funny side to something you may have done that wasn't so good.

Then she would laugh with that cackle only she had!

I can't think of a better person to put this book together than Brad. He is one of the most positive people I know, you can guess who the other is....

I truly think our mom has made anyone she has come in to contact with realize there are positive ways to look at every situation, it's just up to you to DO IT.

Missing you daily,
Leah Dines

STORIES

HERE WE GO

"You're never going to kill storytelling, because it's built into the human plan. We come with it."

— MARGARET ATWOOD

My sister and I were in our early teens when our parents "dragged" us to Europe.

Believe you me, we didn't want to go. We wanted to go to the beach and hang out and bake in the summer sun.

No can do.

One of the worst parts was mom reading old letters from family while we traveled by train.

We had no cell phones (The shock! The horror!) nor anything else to do but look out the window and listen to mom read letters from super old people who had died before we were even born.

I mean, seriously folks, who cares?

We sure didn't.

Yet, here I am, several decades later and I remember about how Uncle Ernst went on and on about the price of corn in Oklahoma and how the rains hadn't come early enough this year and if the family back in Germany was going to emigrate.

Stories.

Storytelling.

It didn't even matter what the content was or who the players were.

It didn't even matter if I was listening (or even actively trying to shut my ears and not listen).

Although I might not have been *listening*, I was *hearing*.

The book you have in your hand is a book of stories. My stories about my mom but also her stories and to my surprise, stories from friends and family that have flooded my inbox in recent weeks as I mentioned I was writing this book.

Some stories are straight from her, too. Writerly guy that I am, I pestered her, I mean, coerced her, no, wait, I reminder her nicely, how great it would be for her to get down some stories about her life.

Especially the ones I didn't know about.

Scattered throughout this book are some of those stories.

I promise I won't get into corn prices during the war.

Repossible

- **Possible:** think about telling the story
- **Impossible:** tell the story when you can no longer speak
- **Repossible:** tell the story (even if they're not "listening," they're "hearing")

STOP AND SAY HELLO

HOW I WISH I HAD KNOWN

"How you do anything is how you do everything."

— T. Harv Eker

When is someone going to name their first child after you?

What needs to happen for that to even be the tiniest thought in someone's mind?

Let's look at a few scenarios:

1. You step in front of her just as an assassin machine guns 20 bullets and you save her life (hopefully, you were wearing a bullet-proof vest). If not, hey, at least you have their first child named after you.
2. You're on the Titanic and there's only one spot left in a life boat. You offer it to her.
3. The planet is erupting with volcanoes and with a burst of adrenaline you carry him to safety.
4. There's a herd of buffalo ...

Or this story below.

"One comment I will never forget. During a class reunion, maybe the 50th, so we were all over 65, a woman came up to me who, frankly, I didn't remember. She said, "I was not very popular in high school and didn't have many friends. But every day, when we came to school, you stopped and said hello to me." Well, I certainly didn't remember that, and I don't think I was all that popular, but I guess she thought I was. She continued, "You were the reason I could start the day with a smile. I named my first child after you." I broke into tears. I am breaking into tears right now as I write this. How I wish I had known at the time what an impact a simple act of kindness could have on someone's day and life."

— DEDE CHARBONNEAU

Repossible

- **Possible:** anything
- **Impossible:** everything
- **Repossible:** stop and say hello

RANDOM ACTS OF KINDNESS
HIDDEN IN YOUR HEART

"Together we can change the world, just one random act of kindness at a time."

— RON HALL

This is a cut and paste from one of mom's stories.

~

"You've probably heard of random acts of kindness. You probably haven't thought about it much. Today I was thinking that there has never been a better time in this world to think about it.

We are all feeing sorry for ourselves right now. With good reason. There has never been a worse disaster to befall our lives. Thousands of people are dying. Sometimes it seems like it is a conspiracy directed at us to keep us from our friends and loved ones! It's impossible to always be reasonable when something so unreasonable happens.

So what am I suggesting? I'm hoping that you can use this

opportunity to turn your focus outward. Maybe just a little bit at a time. Be honest with yourself: when was the last time you did something really nice for someone without being asked and without expecting a thank you or gratitude. Or even acknowledgment.

Let me give you an example. I actually made this an assignment for my seventh graders one year. They had to commit one act of random kindness each day, telling no one, ever. It was darned hard. They were not used to thinking of ways to make other people happy. They were busy enough ensuring their own happiness. And to make it worse, one requirement was that one of these acts had to be for someone they disliked intensely. And they had to report to me in writing each week what they had done and how they felt about it.

Well, I'm not going to go into detail about some of the amazing things that happened. Remember I had a lot of gang-bangers and not-so-nice kids in my class. Their stories were the best.

A wise author once said (happens to be a family member), "What you freely give comes back to you many times over." And if you can somehow make this selfless giving a habit in your life, it's going to come back to you. But you don't do it with the idea that you will be getting something back in return. No payback time. It's hidden in your heart.

So what can you do now, in this time of social isolation to do unplanned kind things for people you love and don't love? I had a hard time thinking of things, to be honest. Since we are isolated with our families, most of these random (unexpected) acts may have to do with family members. Maybe you will think of a whole bunch of things I didn't consider.

So here goes:

1. Put a flower on your mom's pillow (ok to steal from garden)
2. Announce you will be totally responsible for dinner next Thursday.
3. Bake some banana bread and leave a loaf on the porch of a neighbor (anonymous)

4. Ask your dad to go on a bike ride for no reason
5. Surprise your family with snacks while they are watching a movie.
6. Do the laundry without asking anyone. Fold it.
7. Do a chore you never do. If you never wash the dishes, pick them all up after dinner and just start washing.
8. Say "yes" immediately when a parent asks you to do something. (Not always, just occasionally.) Great shock value.
9. Comb your mom's hair
10. Give your dad a shoulder massage when he's looking a little down.
11. Choose a person from your class who doesn't have many friends. Call him/her. Make up some lame excuse if you have to.
12. Call or text your grandmother for no reason.
13. Pick up the dog poop in the yard.
14. Write a note to a teacher who has helped you in some way. Just a little note of appreciation. He/she will never forget it. OK to sign your name.
15. Offer homework help to someone younger than you.
16. Leave a note for your sibling under her/his pillow. Anything positive: Great basketball game today. Thanks for the homework help. Your cookies were great. I'm glad you're my sister/brother. At least today.

MY MOM WAS a teacher for a bazillion years (OK, something like 25). But she only started after my sister and I were off to school, when mom was around 50.

The one of the list above that really hits home is this one:

"Write a note to a teacher who has helped you in some way."

Probably because I know about a story where someone wrote to my mom.

Which brings up the next chapter, how about this for a title: "Write a note to a teacher who has helped you in some way."

Repossible

- **Possible:** think about a random act of kindness you'd like to do (but don't actually do it)
- **Impossible:** feel the impact of giving without having given
- **Repossible:** write a note to a teacher who has helped you in some way

WRITE A NOTE TO A TEACHER WHO HAS HELPED YOU IN SOME WAY

"YOU PROBABLY DON'T REMEMBER ME, BUT…"

"Tell me and I forget. Teach me and I remember. Involve me and I learn."

— BENJAMIN FRANKLIN

om received numerous emails, letters, and Facebook messages that usually started out the same:

"You probably don't remember me, but…"

Or sometimes:

"You probably never noticed me, but…"

Then the note or letter or email would proceed to tell them about a particular day or a span of years where Mrs. Charbonneau did something that:

1. Made them feel noticed
2. Reminded them they were not invisible (no matter how

much they might have tried to hide in the back of the
classroom)
3. Gave them a sense of identity
4. Gave them permission to let their voice be heard
5. Showed them that they felt listened to
6. Proved to them that they felt seen

Can you visualize the classroom? Way in the back? Sometimes the ones trying to hide? So the teacher doesn't call on them?

Those were the best messages my mom got, from those she didn't expect to hear from.

Sometimes, the notes came from the attentive students who went on to university "as expected" they would.

But more often that not, it came from the surprisingly quiet kids who really were hiding out in the back of the classroom yet somehow Mrs. Charbonneau still made them feel included, a part of the class, an active participant in the planet.

In other words, there was no escape from the uplifting Mrs. Charbonneau.

Well, that's only partly accurate. If you really tried to hide, if you were determined not to learn and waste your entire time in middle school, you could very well succeed at it.

But if you were open to the idea of learning, of becoming more than you might have thought possible, of earning a spot in the spotlight of your own personal meaning and purpose?

*"Dear Mrs. Charbonneau, you probably don't remember
me, but..."*

Even if mom didn't remember them, she was living her truth and since "How you do anything is how you do everything." and her anything was giving and teaching and caring and trying and listening, they remembered her.

Then, years later, they wrote her a note.

Did you catch the Random Acts of Kindness chapter? The bullet point about writing a note to a teacher who has helped you in some way?

Should I assign homework here? Due tomorrow by end of class?

No, I have a better idea.

It's due right now.

Here's my challenge.

Pick someone, anyone, a teacher, a mentor, a friend, who has helped you in some way and write them a note.

Let's get the homework assignment straight from the teacher. I'll copy and paste.

> *"Write a note to a teacher who has helped you in some way.*
> *Just a little note of appreciation. He/she will never*
> *forget it. OK to sign your name."*

You don't need to tell anyone. If you can do it anonymously, go for it.

If you'd like to share your note or if you can't track down the person you'd like to contact and you'd just like to get it off your chest, I just commented inside of the Bonus Content for this book at ga. repossible.com. When you're in, look for the entry titled "Write a Note to a Teacher Who Has Helped You in Some Way" and then go leave a comment with your story.

Repossible

- **Possible:** tell me and I forget
- **Impossible:** don't teach me and I remember
- **Repossible:** involve me and I learn

5

ATTITUDE. ARE WE BORN WITH IT OR CAN WE LEARN IT?

"SO, HOW CAN WE BE LIKE DEDE?"

"Motivation will almost always beat mere talent."

— NORMAN RALPH AUGUSTINE

I have the conversation still clearly in my memory. A family member, someone who knew mom since birth, asked:

"So, are you born with that attitude or can you learn it?"

— FAMILY MEMBER

We used to live in San Francisco. We were fans of the basketball team the Golden State Warriors and especially Stephen Curry.

Stephen Curry has talent. Oh boy. Tons of it.

Yet, who is the one who stays after the regular practice and shoots 100 **extra** three-point shots?

Let's do a quick warehousing.

1. He has talent.

2. He is continually learning, improving, practicing (to build on that talent).

Continuing in the sports arena for a moment, taking an example of someone, oh, I don't know, OK fine, me.

I can shoot a basketball. I played high school ball. I was pretty good.

Talent? Sure, I had some.

NBA level? No way.

So could I compete with Steph Curry? Of course not.

But let's get back to attitude, let's bring it down a notch from pro basketball fantasyland to the reality of having a Goddamn Attitude—the kind you want to have, hope to have, dream of having.

What if you're not born with that "attitude" talent?

Can you learn it?

I think, just like Steph, it's going to be easier if you had it in you from the start. But we're talking about a "soft" skill here, a "talent" of having a positive, uplifting, and generous and loving attitude.

The after-practice shots are easier—but still as important.

So can we learn attitude?

I would have to say: absolutely.

Is it easier than becoming a pro basketball player?

Most definitely.

I hear you whispering:

"Gee, this is great, Bradley. I now know how to improve my shot: go shoot more baskets. Awesome possum. But what about, you know, the title of this book? How do I improve my attitude?"

— Maybe You, Maybe Whispering

OK, maybe you wouldn't say *awesome possum*. But you might have whispered the other bit.

Let's get practical.

Repossible

- **Possible:** practice
- **Impossible:** rely only on talent (and don't improve it)
- **Repossible:** practice your talent (even if it's minuscule)

6

—————

THE LITTLE-KNOWN SECRET TO HELPING YOURSELF (AND IMPROVING YOUR ATTITUDE)

HINT: IT HAS LITTLE TO DO WITH YOU

"We are all here on earth to help others; what on earth the others are here for I don't know."

— W. H. AUDEN

If you don't or can't believe this chapter, I completely understand. I can safely say I didn't "get it" until very recently in my life.

But as much as it might be hard to believe, it's true and it works.

Let's say for a moment you're having a bad day. Or let's up the ante a bit and say you're having a bad month. Really bad.

The self-doubt is sitting in the front you while you're naked on stage.

The imposter syndrome is in the press box writing a review of how you shouldn't be on stage. Ever.

You would love nothing more than to run backstage and cry yourself into a puddle of hot tears.

No, it's not a great moment.

You want help. You need help. You need someone to prop you up, lift you to the skies, help you go anywhere but down further.

This is a controversial (and by controversial, I mean the argument between the angel on one of your shoulders and the devil on the other) topic but I'm not only going to stick with it, I'm going to double down on it and go in hard and strong.

One of the best ways to improve your attitude is to **help someone else.**

I know, I know.

I just set the scene with you in a soggy swamp of sorrow and you want help from above—not reaching across or even down below (maybe to someone who's having an even worse month than you are).

Stay with me here.

It was one of the few times I witnessed true sadness from my mother. One of the few times I saw her really cry.

I barely remember it, I was young.

She was sitting on her bed. The carpet was green (and thick!).

I didn't know what to do so I sat next to her.

She was sad.

I didn't know what to feel but I was scared that she was sad and vulnerable.

Even in that state of sorrow and sadness, she managed to console me.

I'm not even sure I needed consoling (I might have just needed a popsicle...) but she lifted herself up lifting me up.

Had I known how to help her, I would have. All I knew how to do was to sit next to her.

She knew what to do.

From that low level, she reached down to me and brought us both up.

Read through the chapter on Random Acts of Kindness if you could use a list of things you could do to lift others up.

Remember, it's fairly easy to help others when you're up, when you're flying high, when you're soaring through the skies on a current that's propelling you even further upwards.

But when you're in that quicksand where every movement seems to pull you further down, see if there's someone you can lift up.

Somehow, in a reverse-gravity, physics-defying act of energy transmission, you are both elevated.

Even if just a little bit.

It's in the right direction.

Help you by helping them.

Repossible

- **Possible:** only help yourself
- **Impossible:** only help others
- **Repossible:** help yourself by helping others

7

—————

READ TO YOUR KIDS

IT DOESN'T HAVE TO INCLUDE CORN PRICES DURING
THE WAR...

"She always gave such good parenting advice and enjoyed talking to my children. We talked about the importance of reading to our kids."

— DAUGHTER OF LONGTIME FRIEND OF THE FAMILY

Friends (and children of friends) have been sending me and my sister snippets and memories from their experiences with mom.

I picked this one (read to your kids) because:

1. It's a difficult one (as the kids get older)
2. I wish I had done it more
3. I want to instill the power of it in you

Often it just takes a simple and short reminder of something to get back into a habit you had been doing but, for whatever reason, aren't do anymore—or as much.

I'm a fan of reading aloud to anyone who wants to listen.

There's a certain magical mysterious sweetness to it that's just not the same as doing other things together with your kids (traveling, watching a movie, bicycling, etc.).

You're telling a story and they're listening.

It's sharing on such a personal and private level, I can't think of anything I'd like to do more with my kids—nor something I would rather have from my parents.

There you have it.

With my admittedly biased perspective, one thing you could take away from this book and do more of.

Read to your kids.

Repossible

- **Possible:** suggest your kids read
- **Impossible:** read while your kids are on their phones and hope they'll "learn by what you're doing"
- **Repossible:** read (aloud) to your kids

8

IT'S THE THOUGHT THAT COUNTS
SCRIBBLED ON A NAPKIN

"Put your heart, mind, and soul into even your smallest acts. This is
the secret of success."

— SWAMI SIVANANDA

I was taking the Amtrak train from Los Angeles to San Francisco
only a few years ago.

Although I no longer attend elementary school, mom
packed me a lunch.

She had a tradition on family car trips of making chicken sandwiches. A bit of mayonnaise, some lettuce, I think there might have
been bit of celery in there for the crunch, salt, quite a bit of pepper,
and on two fresh slices of bread.

The joke was that we often couldn't even wait until the freeway
onramp to open them.

I settled into my window seat on the train and opened my paper
bag lunch.

The chicken sandwich was there. Also a pack of Reese's, an apple,
and a paper towel. Even a bottle of water complete with ice cubes
wrapped around it in a small plastic bag.

The paper towel was sometimes inside of a Ziplock bag to, I don't know, I guess to absorb some of the moisture from the mayonnaise? I don't know—even though to this day, I do the same thing out of habit.

As I opened the sandwich, I saw some color on the paper towel. Maybe it was just the color of the ink of the design on the paper.

No, it was writing.

It said, "I love you. — Mom"

The simplest of messages. Written on a napkin. In a chicken sandwich. On a train.

It was just a note. It wasn't a gift bought at the store. It wasn't complicated. Just a moment of love. Written on a napkin.

These tiny moments matter.

Dare I be so bold to say that these slivers are time are the only things that matter.

As a kid, a son or daughter, depending on how old (or maybe how mature or how experienced) he or she is, we might think that the big gift is what we want and we wouldn't be wrong. At that time, it is what we want.

But later, when the memories come back, when you're, oh, I don't know, writing a book about your mom, what comes back?

Is it the big deal, the fancy event, the expensive gift, the momentous occasion?

Or is it a few words scribbled on a napkin wrapped around a chicken sandwich?

Our gifts are what we make of them, what we offer, and the love with which we give them.

Give love.

And chicken sandwiches.

With a napkin.

And a note.

Repossible

- **Possible:** store bought
- **Impossible:** store bought and unique
- **Repossible:** unique

WITHOUT YOU

WHERE I AM TODAY

"I have come to believe that a great teacher is a great artist and that there are as few as there are any other great artists. Teaching might even be the greatest of the arts since the medium is the human mind and spirit."

— John Steinbeck

Her student wrote me the note below. It would be impossible to calculate the number of people she helped over the years.

Although one thing is certain: it's more than zero.

"Thank you Mrs. Charbonneau for teaching me the English language. Without you I would not be where I am today!"

— Former Student

What if we strove to help only one person in the world? What if that single person said something like the student does above? That we helped them get to where they are today?

If 6 billion people did this for someone else, just 1 person each, that would take care of every single human on the planet.

But then what if you helped 2 people? Or 10 people?

Or every single day for 25 years during 6 classes with 32 kids each?

(I know my dad would want me to calculate that, so here goes.)

25 years X 6 classes X 32 kids = 4,800

She's one person.

What if we all influenced one person?

Repossible

- **Possible:** learn
- **Impossible:** hide
- **Repossible:** teach

10

DON'T BE TOO SURE

IF LIFE ISN'T FULL OF SURPRISES, MAKE YOUR OWN

"Surprise is the greatest gift which life can grant us."

— BORIS PASTERNAK

Keep in mind as you read the short story below that my mom started teaching when she was 50.

If my dad's side of the family (Charbonneau) was the more conservative and serious side, my mom's side (Mall) was the wild and unexpected side.

If I had to choose only one side...

Wait a minute.

Who says we have to choose one side?

Strive for a balance (and not 50-50!) with a bit more of this and some less of that and always, always, keep the surprises coming.

"My favorite story about Dede which I am certain anybody who was there that day will recall, is one day at lunch we were sitting in the office and chatting. We were talking about the growing trend of tattoos and many expressed a disdain for them. Dede said don't be too sure, and stood up pulled down her pants and showed us I believe was a rose tattoo on her hip. Quite a memorable lunch! She spoke of you kids often and was so proud of you."

— TEACHER COLLEAGUE

She very well could have kept quiet and held her secret to herself.

What is the more daring part of us that we sometimes want to set free?

Might it offend someone? Probably.

Will it kill them? Probably not.

Might it be remembered decades later and brought up in a response to an email from the kids of your friend from years back and laughing through telling the story of a friend who was full of surprises? Yep.

You think you know someone. Sure, you probably know them.

But do you know the secrets? The surprises? All of them?

Don't be too sure.

Repossible

- **Possible:** guess
- **Impossible:** know
- **Repossible:** surprise

11

FUN, QUIRKY, BRILLIANT, AND UNAFRAID

I'D TAKE ANY ONE OF THOSE, PLEASE

"Your Mom was so fun, quirky, brilliant and unafraid!"

— FRIEND FROM WAY BACK

I'm reading through the stories that friends and family sent me for our memorial celebration this summer—and for this book.

There are passages, even just parts of sentences that had I not known my mother, would make me wish I had known my mother.

The one who described Dede as the title of this chapter also wrote:

"we all just fell on the bed laughing and giggling"

My mom graduated near the top of her class in university yet "laughing and giggling" would be words that came to me—and to this old friend—first.

The woman who wrote these words, the email to me, I wonder if she spent 10 hours or 10 minutes on the email. Her descriptions seemed so carefully chosen yet I'm going to bet that it was 10 minutes and it just came to her naturally.

If you've read any of my books, you'll know I can't go very long without a numbered list and this chapter merits one.

1. Fun
2. Quirky
3. Brilliant
4. Unafraid

Seriously? All four? I would be happy if someone described me with any one of those adjectives.

But all of them? In one package?

How could this old friend have remembered such a collection of characteristics and then lay them out so effortlessly?

1. **Fun:** I write about Fun Money in another chapter and it's an integral part of her personality. Maybe because she had the *brilliant* taken care of, fun came more easily. In fact, I bet they're related although I wonder if *brilliant* people always know how to let the fun shine through.
2. **Quirky:** this is definitely a Mall (maiden name) trait. Mom's side of the family is the one who wants to dress up in wild costumes on Halloween (or, frankly, any time of the year). Dad thought it was all silly and, usually, embarrassing. See point #4.
3. **Brilliant:** remember, these aren't my descriptions (although I wish they had been). This goes beyond schooling and education. I like words such as clever or quick witted. But she had brilliant down pat.
4. **Unafraid:** interesting that this is the last one because by my calculations here, it can be difficult to be unafraid if you're not having fun and brilliant. Sure, you can be unafraid because you're naïve or just don't know you

should be afraid but to be fun and brilliant and then unafraid is a delightful and enviable position.

Unafraid

If you're reading this book (which is a trick question, of course!), you might be thinking:

> *"What is this book anyway? Some glory story (ooh, I just made that up: glory story) about this author's mother?"*

Yep, sure, you could say that.

But I'm going to inherit at least one of these character traits from mom and if they're not already in my blood or my genes, I'm going to learn them or even force them.

I could apologize for this chapter (or this entire book). I could write disclaimers to the tone of, "Hey, this book is full of love for my mom and if you don't like it (or if you don't get any benefit from it), I'm sorry."

I could do that.

But I'm going to take that unafraid trait and run with it.

They say on your deathbed you mostly regret what you didn't do rather than what you did.

I'm 100% certain I won't regret having written a book about my mom. Even when it's a *glory story*.

In fact, instigator that I am, rabble rouser that my mom was, and motivational mutt that I strive to be, I'm going to challenge you to write a book about your mother.

There, I said it.

When I started this book, I was wondering if I would suggest that somewhere in the book and here it is.

Remember the train rides and the old letters from dead people? Reading can be therapeutic. But writing? I'd go as far as to remove the "can be" and state that writing *is* therapeutic.

Let's say you didn't even like your mom. Or you didn't know her well. You might think you don't have anything to write about.

I challenge that you do.

Even what you don't know, the stories you heard, even as far as the imagination you might have built up over the years.

Oh, let's not forget dad. You can write about him, too.

But as far as being unafraid to write this chapter? This book? Unafraid to challenge you to write your own book about your own mother?

I won't be on my deathbed regretting much I didn't do.

Because I'm doing it.

Because I'm striving to be fun, quirky, brilliant, and unafraid.

Which of those are you?

Which do you strive to become?

What other characteristics do you strive towards?

I just had a conversation with a student in my "How to Write Your Worst Book Ever" course and she and I talked about hosting a memoir workshop.

I had just two requirements for the potential course students: ideally, the book is *short*, and, related to that, they have to get it *done*.

I'm going to take a gamble here and ponder the idea that if we are unafraid or at least daring to take a chance, might fun, quirky, and brilliant come to us more effortlessly?

Repossible

- **Possible:** fun
- **Impossible:** brilliant and unafraid
- **Repossible:** fun, quirky, brilliant, and unafraid

12

FUN MONEY

YOU CAN'T USE THIS TO PAY THE ELECTRICITY BILL

"If you obey all the rules you miss all the fun."

— KATHARINE HEPBURN

Mom and dad taught us quite a bit about finances, money, budgeting, and investing.

I often took the *saving* aspect a little too far.

I often don't make rational decisions in the traditional sense of *regular* or *socially-accepted* pros and cons.

- I pursued an international MBA degree so I could eventually move to Europe.
- I traveled hours on a train alone in Poland to a place called Hel so I could say I've been to Hel—and back.
- I chose to study German in the freshly-opened East Germany because it sounded more difficult and exotic.

But with money, sometimes it went a little too extreme.

When I was planning on going to France for my junior year abroad during university, I calculated that I could go for an extra two weeks in the summer if I stayed at nicer places and did normal touristy stuff.

However, I reckoned if I could find a place to stay that cost less and I could get a special visa that would allow me to work and ate ten-Franc pizza on a regular basis, I could stay for two months.

Two weeks or two months living in Paris?

Yet, two weeks of (relative) luxury or two months of going Full-On Traveler Mode?

The young adventurer that I was, it was an easy decision. It was more of a decision to try to stop me from staying three months.

But mom also wanted me to not live completely like a *clochard* (one of my favorite words in French).

Occasionally, she sent me (and I highly discourage this!) cash in envelopes with the mail.

However, there were strict guidelines and regulations attached to these funds.

I wasn't allowed to spend it on anything rational or boring or administrative.

I had to spend it on something fun, silly, or just out of character.

The *veritable clochard* that I was, this was quite a challenge for me. I thought much more, "Ooh, with this money, I could extend my stay here for another week!"

But alas.

The rule-follower that I usually am, I adhered to her rules and spent it on something fun.

Let's take this apart for a moment.

My mom wanted to make sure I was having fun. She wanted to guarantee I would do silly things for no reason and enjoy it.

Sure, she probably sent letters about how I should study and get good grades and be nice to old ladies crossing the street. She must have.

But what do I remember?

Fun money.

What if we took this attitude and shared it, distributed even the smallest molecule of it with those we love?

Sure, we want our friends and family to succeed, do good in the world, and all that. Yep, I get it.

But how often do we not only allow but encourage people to really just have fun?

Maybe even more than encourage, but demand.

If you can't think of someone else to sprinkle a little of this fun money on, try it on yourself.

A few years later, OK, fine, many years later and I'd still rather live in Paris for two months than two weeks but that's the true traveler who lives in my heart.

But somewhere, after paying the boring bills and making sure I have enough to eat, I force myself to spend money on completely oddball adventures and toast my mom for making certain we have fun in our lives.

Especially if it comes in the form of cash in an envelope from the other side of the planet.

Repossible

- **Possible:** pay the electricity bill
- **Impossible:** spend the fun money on the electricity bill but then later use the same amount of money for fun— and have the same effect
- **Repossible:** fun money

13

"I HATE READING"

"I PROMISE I WILL TRY TO CHANGE THAT FOR YOU"

"I don't care what you read. Just read."

— MY DAD

T his chapter I'm cutting and pasting from something mom wrote. *Enjoy.*

"I HATE READING," one of my seventh graders announced to the class. "Me, too," responded some others. I looked at them like they had told me their favorite dog had just died.

"I am so so sorry," I truthfully told them. "I promise I will try to change that for you. I will feel awful if I send you out into life without the comfort and joy of books." They were extremely scornful of my comments, but I was determined to sway as many minds as possible.

Kids hate reading because they can't read because they don't read. It is a vicious circle. I started by reading fun books aloud to the whole class. (And these were seventh graders, 15 years old, not second graders.) I promised I wouldn't bore them with more than one chapter a day. Eventually, my fidgety audience started to focus. As I would close the book after a chapter, they would beg: "Just one more chapter!" "Oh, no, I wouldn't do that to you. I promised not to bore you to death." We then graduated from my reading to listening to an audio tape with a capable narrator, while they followed along line by line in the book. I just hope that somehow the hook was set and reading became a positive experience for them.

But when I see adults who don't read, I am sad for them, too. I remember being on jury duty: eight hours sitting in a chair waiting for a possible assignment which usually didn't come. Fortunately, I had a great book and a pillow and I was set for the day. I looked at the lady next to me. She was doing a word search. A word search. Is there anything so mindless. I was so sorry for her. Reading can help you learn stuff, sure, but it is also a total escape, a way out of a world you don't want to be in at the moment. You want to wimp out of a bad situation, put your nose in a book.

I'm not worried about my grandchildren. All four of you are competent and often enthusiastic readers. When I think of Luca, I think of him reading a book, even a Donald Duck comic in Dutch. I looked through one of his comics and was quite amazed at the elevated vocabulary in the little bubbles. He had no idea how much he was expanding his language. He was just having fun.

My kids, Brad and Leah, were not avid readers through school. How embarrassing since I was an English teacher. They were just not interested unless a book was assigned and they had to read it. Basically, they were determined not to enjoy it.

In Brad's case, he started reading because he had nothing else to do. After high school, he set off on a European jaunt with a friend and found himself at one point on a Greek island with not much to do except gaze at the blue ocean (and the girls, probably). He started reading. He didn't just read books, he devoured stacks of them. With Leah, I can't pinpoint the time, but all of a sudden, probably after she was married, she was never without a book. Her idea of a great evening was often to get into her jammies and read her book.

But the biggest convert was BJ. I can still picture it. He was determined to be the best father ever. He knew that the kids would do what they saw the parents doing, not what the parents told them to do. And that, he realized, applied to reading. I remember the scene. He positioned the girls on the floor on a blanket in front of his rocking chair. Making sure they were paying attention, he got out his book and started reading. I truthfully don't remember him ever reading a book before that time, but since then, I don't think I have ever seen him without a book.

Not all parents have this insight. We have a friend with three cute daughters in elementary school. They do not read books. Their mother told us they have a better way of "enjoying literature." They go to movies. About three a week. It is much more fun than reading, she explained. As might be expected, all three attend remedial reading classes at their school and have limited vocabularies.

You don't have to read stuff that doesn't interest you to reap the rewards of reading. It's called "recreational reading." That means it's fun. You are not looking up facts for a research paper. I remember plowing through Winston Churchill's History of England. I even took it when I went into labor with Brad. Figured it would put me to sleep. And they took it away from me! I never understood the logic of that.

What am I asking you to do, anyway? Include reading in your daily routine. Hide away in a corner for half an hour and decompress. Put the screens and video games to the side for a while. Technology is a big part of our lives now, and games are fun to play. But they are limiting, and your brain needs a chance to expand. Don't give up those fun diversions, just add some books to the mix. Keep an eye out for books that seem interesting. They are so accessible now through Kindle and your other devices, and they can be delivered to these great gadgets free from your library. I don't know if kids have book clubs, but that would be a new way to connect. Probably online, making new friends and exploring new ideas. Why not.

Just for the sake of your own ego, remember you are judged by how you talk. (Read the book Pygmalion by George Bernard Shaw made into a movie My Fair Lady. It's about a professor who teaches a street flower-seller to speak such proper English that people are convinced she is a princess.) If you only talk with friends and have no access to an expanded vocabulary through books, you will always sound like a sixth grader. Sort of like our current president. TV and movies are written with a fifth grade vocabulary in mind. Documentaries and science programs, etc. are aimed at a higher audience. But nothing comes close to what you painlessly get from reading real books.

Don't forget the so-called classics. They have been around a long time for a reason. If you don't have a nodding acquaintance with Shakespeare or Dickens, many people are going to think you are pretty ignorant. Google a list of famous books and check them out.

And remember, if you don't read, you'll never be able to write. We get our writing models from our reading. Writing, even though we rely on texting and email for short thoughts, is still essential in the business world and global communication. If you can write succinctly and clearly, you will be in demand. Grandpa liked to tell the story of how he hired high-level, Phd engineers. He would take a look at their high-powered resumes, then ask them to turn the paper over and write a paragraph about something, like what they hoped to accomplish in the job. If what they wrote was comprehensible, grammatically correct, understandable and literate, he would hire them. If not, he sent them on their way. He said if they couldn't speak and write well, he would have to write all their reports for them.

I had a kid in seventh grade who really brought this point home for me. She was constantly reading a book in class. While I was talking. I would ask her to put it down and listen to the lesson and do her assignment. She would go along with that for a little bit, and then return to her book. I finally gave up. I told her to take her book and sit in the back where she wouldn't be noticed. Whatever happened, happened. She could take the consequences. And what were the consequences? She achieved the highest score of any seventh grader in the school on English standardized tests.

So if you do nothing else, if you drop out and end up on the streets, just keep reading.

Repossible

- **Possible:** watch movies
- **Impossible:** watch movies (and get the same benefits as reading)
- **Repossible:** read

14

MOST OF US HAD NEVER _______ BEFORE

AFTER THAT, I BECAME A REGULAR

"Ideas pull the trigger, but instinct loads the gun."

— DON MARQUIS

I didn't quite realize the extent my mom was a rabble rouser.

When there was forced busing in schools in Los Angeles, she organized a group of parents to take action.

Even in her final years, she said she would create the directory for the place she lived (with 80 people) and she ended taking over the project but the real reason she wanted to do it was so she could take pictures of everyone and then give her an excuse to get to know them and especially those who didn't want to be gotten to know.

But it goes way back.

"We both had younger daughters, similar in age. Dede convinced me to change my daughter to Leah's preschool. It was the Sherman Oaks Cooperative preschool. She knows how to gently persuade people!

At one parent meeting, a mother announced that her husband

had leukemia, and needed blood. Within days, Dede organized a "Blood donation/Pot Luck lunch" at her house. Most of us had never donated blood before. After that, I became a regular donor. I was type o-negative (universal donor) plus am one of 15% of the population that can donate to premature babies. So Dede provided the Red Cross with a long time donor!"

— Elementary School Parent and Longtime Friend

My sister and I are also instigators. I think we take the "What's the worst that could happen?" approach and weigh that against "What's the best that could happen?" and make the decision from there.

But daring to take that initial action, not wait for a consensus or even collaboration, but just taking the action.

People are drawn to leaders because they lead. They take the first step then look back, proclaim the coast is (probably) clear, and wave in the troops.

Take a moment to read again what her friend wrote:

"Most of us had never _____ before."

And then what happened thanks to that initial action (the reaction):

"I became a regular _____."

What's the worst that could have happened?

- No one wanted to give blood.
- Their friend died.

What's the best?

- They gave blood.
- Maybe they helped their friend live.

It's not just being nice or active or thoughtful (although that's part of it). What I like about this story is that maybe it was a case of, with the right attitude, it was a matter of life and death.

Repossible

- **Possible:** give
- **Impossible:** give to dare
- **Repossible:** dare others to give

15

IN MY HEART SHE LIVES FOREVER

SHE GAVE ME HOPE FOR A BETTER LIFE

"A life is not important except in the impact it has on other lives."

— Jackie Robinson

Mom heard a woman speak about a cause where she helped kids in other countries get through school. She liked it because it was directly through the connection with this woman that she could trust the organization behind it. Unfortunately, charities get a bad rap because of a handful of scumbags who scam funds and ruin the goodness of the original idea

But help kids get through school? Yep, that will work.

Of course, in true Dede Charbonneau fashion, sending off some monetary support on a regular basis wasn't quite going to cut it.

Eventually, she connected with her student and they started an email correspondence that went on for years.

I don't know if he knows it, but mom read us his emails on a regular basis. His name became almost as much a part of the family as the names Liam, Luca, Maddie, and Taylor.

There are so many emails from him. There are so many emails from her.

This last one he wrote to my sister gives you an idea of what it means to do that little bit more, to send not just monetary support but emails and questions, notes and answers, responses and curiosity.

"Not a single day passes by when I don't miss her .miss her letters of encouragement...So I think you all there should organize a party...So that we can All share in her good memories...Even though I'll not be there...to attend...I want you all to know....am with you...I have always been with you..all. Dede was a blessing in my life...She gave me hope for a better life ...She changed my life... forever...and for that in my heart she lives forever."

— MOM'S FRIEND IN AFRICA

When I first started writing this book, I thought it was just going to be a few fun stories about mom. Maybe I'd make fun of her giant, red-rimmed glasses. Or try to describer her cackling laugh. Or pretend I could learn or study as well as she did.

What I didn't really expect was to cry throughout the second half of most of the chapters of this book.

Of course, it's a beautiful thing. But on the other hand, it also puts some pressure on us kids. How can we fill such shoes? Did she really mean so much to all of these people? How did she do it? How can we rustle up a fraction of her energy, her altruism, her generosity?

He says above:

"She changed my life... forever...and for that in my heart she lives forever."

I mean, seriously here, folks. Sure, I think mom is great and all but she's got people naming their children after her and she's changing lives and living in the hearts of *people she never even met in person* forever.

How are we supposed to compete with that?!

We're not.

Because it's not a competition.

It's a cooperation. A collaboration.

In fact, it's not a zero-sum game. If mom gave lots of her attention or love to someone else, somehow, although mathematically it doesn't make sense, it actually grows the attention or love.

In a linear world, a simple construction where you start with 10 apples, if you give me 1 apple, you now have 1 less, you have 9.

Yet with attention, love, and dare I say, even money, not all mathematical rules apply.

Her love for her faraway student somehow didn't take away from the love she gave us kids.

Although seemingly against all of the laws of physics, her actions grew the entirety of love.

I'd like to thank her friend in Africa because he has just helped me get to the next chapter which has been brewing in my mind for days and has been looking for a place to land: Love is Not a Zero-Sum Equation.

Repossible

- **Possible:** send money
- **Impossible:** send money and hope to make a connection (only through the sending of money)
- **Repossible:** make a lasting, true connection

16

LOVE IS NOT A ZERO-SUM EQUATION
IT GROWS EXPONENTIALLY

"The real energy occurs in each connection between two people, which can bring about exponential returns."

— TOM RATH

Do you ever hear or read something that makes sense but then only later does it really sink in and hit you? Then it hits you hard and you think, "Oh man, this is good. No, this is really good."

Maybe it's a writer thing—or a creator thing.

I'm usually working on a book and pretty much any thought that passes through my mind is potential fodder for material. However, not everything sticks (thankfully!) but the really good stuff doesn't go away—even if you want it to do.

Then you need to write it down.

Then a chapter comes along about seemingly something else and it triggers this new chapter.

This is one of those chapters.

Sharing Grows the Whole

I wish I could remember the podcast or audiobook I was listening to. I don't remember who said it or even the details. But here's the gist.

He used a digital file as a metaphor for how something can begin as a single element or entity and grow.

In the case of the digital file, let's take a music file, it begins its existence as a single file sitting on a server somewhere.

When you download that file, you are not taking from the original fie, you are making a copy of it. Now there are two. Yet nothing was taken away from the original file, it is still intact and whole.

Yet you now have the same file, a complete duplicate that is nothing less or more than the original, yet the original still also exists.

Of course, this can happen again and again. Even your music file can be shared (careful here, I'm not proposing illegal file sharing!).

So the piece of music (or book or video) is now in the hands of multiple people and yet the original file is none the worse (or better) for it.

Got it? Good.

Now let's replace that digital file with:

- love
- attention
- learning
- caring
- listening
- asking
- _______ (fill in the blank)

Let's keep it simple and pick one: love.

Love is not a zero-sum element. It's not like a pie or 10 apples where if you take one away, the original is lessened.

Love is not a regular player in the mathematical equations. Not only does it bend the rules, it seems to break them with glee.

You might think that with something like love, if she gives more to him than to me, I get less. It might seem that way. But it's not the case.

Even mom's story of her friend in Africa can add to the pie. The pie just keeps getting bigger. There is no limit to the expanse of love. Her love for him is another download. It doesn't take away from her love for me (or my sister or her grandkids). In fact, it adds to it. Each action, each showing of love, is another download, another copy, another full file full of love that was born into the world.

We might think there is a ceiling or a barrier or a maximum.

There is not.

There is so much love.

Giving begets more giving.

Love brings more love.

There is no end.

There is only beginning.

If you choose, it starts with you.

Repossible

- **Possible:** bake a pie
- **Impossible:** take from the pie
- **Repossible:** grow the pie

17

"WE'RE TERRIBLY SORRY, MS. MALL, BUT ..."

THE BIRTH OF EVERY SINGLE DAY

"The secret of your future is hidden in your daily routine."

— MIKE MURDOCK

"No, dad, not that story! Not again!"

It's true. I've told this story to my kids so many times it's become a family joke.

Because you, dear reader, are not my kids, I'm going to indulge you in this first (and probably not last) telling of the story.

Before I begin, I'm going to make another push for writing your mom's (and/or dad's) story. A biography, if you will, but then shorter. Even just a few snippets. Maybe a collection of stories, even just the ones you remember. Like this book.

I wish I had my mom here so she could properly tell this story in her own words and without the embellishments I will certainly add as I dig back to try to remember the details.

See what I mean? See how it would be better, easier, and

not to mention more fun to write someone else's story
when they're still around to help you tell it?

My mother was an excellent student. Yet she was the first to state that it wasn't a question so much of intelligence as it was of habits, rituals, and persistence.

She also knew how to have fun. Well, "knowing how" to have fun doesn't mean you have fun, I suppose, so let me rephrase and say she knew how to have fun and she had fun.

Lots of fun.

She went to all of the parties and the events in university. She would be out late at night and yet still make the sporting event the next day.

She had a secret weapon. But I'll get to that in a minute.

At her university, there were sororities and fraternities. If you're not familiar with this phenomenon in the United States, they are social groups at the schools to encourage making friends (even life-long friends), having fun, and also learning life skills outside of the classroom.

Today, they get some bad press as they are known for their excessive partying but back in the day, they were more reputable and it was an honor to be selected to join.

Speaking of which, that's how it works: you're invited to join a sorority (women) or a fraternity (men).

There is enormous pressure to be in this sorority or that one. They have their types and stereotypes, their clichés and their reputations.

There are parties and an elaborate evaluation process that's probably harder to get in than the school itself—or at least as much pressure.

Young Ms. Mall attended all the parties. In fact, maybe she attended a few too many of the parties. Maybe she was just a little too gung-ho and partook in a smidgen too many of the festivities.

When there was a big exam on Monday, she might be seen going out to dinner or out with friends—but not in the library studying, where she should be!

She didn't cram for the tests, she didn't stress about her grades, and she wasn't seen often enough in the late-night study sessions.

She was seen as something of a party girl—and, in the purview of the sororities, just didn't take her academics seriously enough.

The clubs are not based solely on your ability to party down but, especially back in those days, they wanted a certain, dare I say, class of person. You not only needed to be social and responsible but get good grades and ideally you were also an upstanding member of society at large.

Again, it was an honor to be chosen by a sorority and much more so those that had the "best" reputations.

Poor Ms. Mall. Apparently, she was seen as having a little too much fun and was, most probably, failing out of half her classes because how could anyone be such a socialite and still get good grades?

When the decision came to invite her or not, the sorority high-lighted that although Ms. Mall was a social rockstar, she was not up to the caliber of academic excellence that this particular sorority wanted to be associated with.

She was not invited to join.

Come report card day, there was a bit of a surprise.

Although not for Ms. Mall.

She had scores and grades that put her around the top of her class. The entire school, actually. As she had expected. As she had been working towards all along.

The secret to her success was not in the late-night study sessions and especially not being a part of the last-minute cram sessions.

No, that would have defeated the purpose, the entire, deeply-rooted strategy of just a little bit on a daily basis.

It wasn't all-night Sunday.

It was 15 minutes extra in the morning. Every single morning.

It wasn't squeezing all of the chapters of the books she hadn't read yet. She had already read them all—every single day making a little progress and deepening her long-term memory as opposed to the short bursts into her short-term memory during cram sessions.

So when the day arrived—and oh, did it arrive—when the sorority reversed their decision and retroactively chose to invite Ms. Mall to their esteemed club, she stated, rather publicly, that this sorority was *not up to the caliber of academic excellence that this particular student wanted to be associated with.*

It is with tremendous pride that I think of her story and how, every single morning for more than seven years, I had a daily writing practice which lay seed to my author career and how, with an odd sense of ease, the book in your hands is my 31st book.

It is no coincidence that the book at the core of my entire writing career is titled "Every Single Day."

Sure, I learned a few things in school. But I learned the most from this one story from my mom.

She didn't need (or even want) the big spotlight. She didn't need to be in the headlines (although she was). But if you challenged her and she took you up on that challenge, let's just say you better have done your homework because chances are excellent that she did hers —and you would hear about it in the end.

Possibly quietly, probably painfully, and certainly you'd never forget it.

Repossible

- **Possible:** cram for exams on Sunday night
- **Impossible:** study while partying
- **Repossible:** build tiny progress every single day

18

A LOOKER

IRREPRESSIBLE ENERGY

"There is no definition of beauty, but when you can see someone's spirit coming through, something unexplainable, that's beautiful to me."

— LIV TYLER

What is beauty? What is attractive? What matters?

"I feel qualified to add this. In high school, in the 50s, Dede was what we called in those days, a "Looker." I'll wager that any young man attending Po-Hi in those days would agree. And it wasn't just because she was a very attractive girl---it was also because of the irrepressible energy that was such an appealing part of who she was."

— HIGH SCHOOL CLASSMATE

The other day, my 15-year-old son said something about some

reality show and how the people on there were "conventionally attractive."

I don't know where he gets his vocabulary—but it's often a surprising choice of words, especially since he doesn't even speak English in his day-to-day life here in The Netherlands and gets his English from YouTube, Netflix, and PlayStation. (Yeah, I know.) We don't even speak English in our house yet he'll toss in some English words in the middle of a Dutch sentence and somehow it all just works.

So let's say for a moment that mom was *conventionally attractive.* Great. Whatever.

Remember the chapter on talent and practice? Born with it and/or build it?

If you're born *conventionally attractive*, maybe like Stephen Curry, does that mean you'll have an easier time with *energy* or even better, with *irrepressible energy*?

What's been surprising about writing this book and especially inviting mom's friends to participate, is to learn a bit about what she was like before I was even born.

Although I wouldn't have used those exact words, I could easily say mom had an irrepressible energy. This means she had it in high school and still had it much later in life.

"The phrase "correlation does not imply causation" refers to the inability to legitimately deduce a cause-and-effect relationship between two events or variables solely on the basis of an observed association or correlation between them."

— WIKIPEDIA

I was trying to explain this idea to my oldest son the other day (and I failed miserably...) but this is a good example.

Mom:

1. Was *conventionally attractive*

2. Had *irrepressible energy*

What the logic is referring to is the causation and/or correlation.

Did she have *irrepressible energy* **because** she was *conventionally attractive* (causation) or did she happen to have both and they weren't necessarily caused by the other (correlation)?

Remember back to that same chapter where my family member asked in Zoom call if mom was born with her attitude or if she learned it.

I feel like I'm making a Ph.D. thesis out of this (hmm, it's not a bad idea...I've been thinking about going back to school) but dare I be so bold as to state that this is possibly one of the most important elements of this entire book?

Attitude: are you born with it or can you learn it?

Apparently, and according even to high school friends, she had both the *altitude* and the *attitude*.

Back in the attitude chapter, we were talking about being born with that attitude yet here we're talking about being born with (or without) something else (attractiveness).

I'm feeling a numbered list of questions coming on...

1. What other factors are there then that contribute to your attitude?
2. How much of that is your genes and how much environmental?
3. How can we identify those factors and (try our best to) influence them?
4. How much can we change?
5. Are you stuck (for better or worse) with how you were in high school?
6. If we'd like to change, how do we go about it?

Let's say we were born with with, to quote my son again but then alter it, *conventional looks*. So we're average. The mathematician in me (yes, I also take after my dad) sees many (oh so many) things in life in the form of charts and/or line graphs.

Let's say we're at the intersection of the X and Y axis. Or let's spice things up a bit and add a third dimension, Z, which will be time.

If X is the "other factor" and Y is attitude (and/or *energy*) and Z is time, how much weight can we attribute to our own influence over the X factor?

> *SIDEBAR: I'm laughing now as I type this as I can hear you, dear reader, possibly whispering to yourself, "Wow, we went from 'she was pretty in high school' to we're actually back in high school mathematics and logic class and this author has me seeing three-dimension line graphs that are going to project the altitude of my future attitude. What's going on here!?"*

If we needed a legend in this graph, what could be the values of X?

If we just take mom here for a moment to try to keep this simple ("Too late!"), what might we have:

1. Physical (looks, conventionally attractive, etc.); exterior
2. Interior (thoughts, feelings, emotions)
3. Family
4. Friends
5. Environment (school, work, location, culture, etc.)
6. Altruism

This is not meant to be an exhaustive list by any means and "altruism" just popped in there as I went through other chapters to add to the list.

If there's one thing I try to sprinkle onto my kids, it's this one that I learned both from my mother and my mother-in-law. It's possibly the best little-known secret to your own happiness.

Could it be that simple?

What if were easy?

It couldn't have been that in high school, she was already thinking of others and that made her so *attractive*, could it? I don't know. I can't know. I don't know if she knew.

Let's do another little inventory of attitude-related traits or actions mentioned in this book (which means, there are probably more I don't know about):

1. Teaching
2. Paying attention
3. Listening
4. Laughing (with you)
5. Giving (gifts, time, thought, love)
6. Random acts of kindness
7. Say hello
8. Unafraid

Could this be a shopping list towards a better attitude?

We started this chapter off with *beauty*.

We're ending up with *unafraid altruism*.

Altruism, thinking of others, is one of those oddballs of physics that doesn't make sense. The math equations don't add up.

$1 + 1 > 2$

One act of altruism plus one other person is greater for both parties involved.

We all benefit. We all benefit exponentially.

Can we do it? Can you do it? What does it mean to *do it*? What if it just meant something as simple as a random act of kindness?

Repossible

- **Possible:** beauty
- **Impossible:** define beauty
- **Repossible:** energy

Another quote from her friend:

"Beauty equals aliveness. Aliveness is beauty in its most attractive form.

That is certainly Dede. And she was always that way. Shakespeare described her in a sonnet: 'For as you were when first your eye I ey'd, Such seems your beauty still.'"

19

THE TRAVELING $1,000+ FRENCH HAUTE COUTURE DRESS

SHARE THE STORIES THAT DON'T HAVE ANY PERSONAL MEANING, TOO

"Storytelling is not what I do for a living - it is how I do all that I do while I am living.

— DONALD DAVIS

One of the my favorite parts of putting this book together has been the stories we're receiving that I didn't know about.
I think I had heard this one but I didn't know the details.
I'll let mom's friend fill you in.

"Margie, our Bohemian artist friend bought the dress in a brown paper bag for $1 at an auction. Margie then gave Dede the dress who immediately wore it to a fancy party. One of Dede's friends saw her and yelled "THAT'S A LEONARDO and yours has an autographed scarf. I paid over $1,000 for a Leonardo dress and it is not as nice as yours. How much did you pay for this?" Dede calmly said "$1."

For the next 30 years Dede and I traded the dress back and forth. Now I am left to carry on the Leonardo Haute Couture dress tradition. I love wearing the dress and feel a connection with Dede and Margie when I wear it. I sent a picture of myself in the dress the day Dede passed away. Leah (Dede's daughter) said Dede loved the picture and kept asking to see it. The Leonardo company is still in business in France and the vintage dress is listed at $1,000."

— Mom's Partner in Fashion Crime

You never know what is going to trigger a life-long memory in someone. However, have you ever noticed that adventure stories never go like this:

1. We went to the place.
2. It was fine.
3. All went as planned.
4. We came home.

The best stories, the most memorable ones, happen when things don't go as planned, when the unexpected takes over, and you go with it, accept it, even embrace it.

Wear the $1 dress to the party. Dare to own the character. Keep the adventure alive by telling the story.

Repossible

- **Possible:** live the stories
- **Impossible:** hide the stories
- **Repossible:** tell the stories

20

ROULETTE

PIÑA COLADAS, ANGELS, AND NUMBER 17

"If you knew who walked beside you at all times, on the path that you have chosen, you could never experience fear or doubt again."

— WAYNE DYER

I could make this chapter really short and tell you about my mom and my mother-in-law at the roulette table but the significance of the scene would be lost without the background story. Here we go.

Dearest Reader,

In the tech world, there's a thing called an Easter egg. It's when inside of an application or a program or a game, there's something special, secret, and often completely out of place that's been hidden there by the creators.

You usually can't read about it in the manual, can't find the instructions on how to locate it anywhere in their official literature, and it often it sneaks up on you out of the blue and brings on a smile and a thought of, "Wait a minute, what's that doing in here? It's out of place, it doesn't really belong here, yet, maybe it does, and maybe this is the best part."

Dare I say that the Easter egg might be this chapter.

I have now "lost" both my parents. In the classical sense, there is no one left I need to impress, no parental figure I need to be on my best behavior for, and certainly now I'm allowed to stay up past my bedtime and do what I really, really want to do.

What comes below here isn't something I had planned or even knew existed, but, like the Easter egg, it appeared to me and it has altered my deep perspective on life—and death.

Are you ready?

This is your last warning. If you only know me, Mr. Author here, Bradley, as the guy who writes every day, travels quite a bit, and sneaks in math equations while playing basketball with his kids, you're in for a treat—or a shock. Or both.

Here we go.

When my dad was diagnosed with cancer, I searched far and wide for anything to help, to save him, to heal his cancer. Had I been convinced that we needed to travel to Brazil to meet some medicine man, I would have bought the plane tickets. Had he needed to eat steamed broccoli for six days with a shot of Tequila chaser, I would have joined him.

I would have—and did—anything I could within my power.

What I learned was that it wasn't *my power* I was searching for— yet that's what I found.

I dare even write it as *my power* because it's not mine. It's not yours. It's ours. We all have access to it.

Although this book is about my mom, it was my dad who started me on this path of discovery but also guided me towards certain directions and away from others.

For example, he was the conservative in the family. He was an engineer, a mathematician, and wanted to see the reports and the peer-reviewed studies supporting whatever it was we were presenting.

Although I could read the books, study the gurus, and listen attentively to the testimonials of miracle healing experiences from people for whom it truly had happened, I felt that in order to convince my dad we had the power to heal our own bodies, I first needed to convince someone far more skeptical, terribly more stubborn, and probably one of the toughest people we can even try to change the mind of.

I needed to first convince myself.

Although we as a society often say how important the perspective and opinions and beliefs of others are to us, we are most often our most critical and harshest judges.

Convincing me was going to be even more difficult than convincing my dad that there was a higher power, something else out there—or in here—that could do things like heal cancer.

In order to walk the talk and learn by doing (is there really any other way to learn?), I would have gone so far as to do a insane-asylum-sounding, 10-day, silent, Vipassana meditation retreat. *Oh wait, I did that.*

I would have traveled to participate in 4-day meditation intensive workshops complete with walk-from-the-hotel-at-three-in-the-morning-through-the-snow-to be-on-time-for-the-four-am meditation with a hall full of strangers. *Yep, did a bunch of those.*

Or maybe do 5-day water-only fasting challenges in search of a cleansing and crystal clarity of my consciousness. *Oops, I found it.*

Perhaps I would have to take up a *meditation practice* and follow it so rigorously as if the doctor prescribed a *medication practice. Uh, yep, did that, doing that.*

I always had my dad in mind and that he would want to see the results, the numbers, and the science behind the seance.

> Ooh, I just wrote that because I like alliteration but I'm
> sticking with it: the science behind the seance.
> Have I mentioned yet how writing brings out in us
> what we don't yet know? Have I droned on and on
> how, without writing it down, I would know next to
> nothing about the anything I experienced first
> hand? Anyway, I'm feeling frisky this morning as I

type these words and come up with witty alliteration.

Only recently have I learned, among the overwhelming styles and types of meditation, that I see it in two main types: passive and active.

I started with passive because I didn't know any better but later discovered I had unconsciously become more of an active meditator.

In other words, it's not sitting there with your eyes closed, hoping to achieve inner peace, banishing all thoughts from your overactive mind, and focusing on your breath. Although those are all great, usually impossible (Banishing all thoughts? Yeah, good luck with that …), it's like watching the replay of the basketball game on TV as compared with being the scoring point guard on the court.

It's the difference from being in the audience of the live theater production as compared with being on stage and/or being in the mind of the playwright who's guiding the action.

I went from being a passive participant in my meditation to more of an active player.

Do you know how in your dreams, usually, you don't have too much control about what's going on—much less your own actions. There's a phenomenon called lucid dreaming where, although you're still fully asleep, you gain a more active role in your dreams and can even direct the show to some extent.

What's really cool about lucid dreaming is that you can get better at it with practice. Meditation, like lucid dreaming, is something you can get better at with practice.

From the guy who wrote the book about daily habits called "Every Single Day" and based on mom's secret study techniques as showcased in the sorority chapter, I take practice very seriously and have a deep respect for making even the tiniest smidgen of progress on a regular basis.

It's 2021 as I write this. I started all this around 2014. I have meditated almost every single day since. As one of my chapters is not called Practice Makes Perfect but rather Practice Is Perfect.

Are you ready for the roulette table?

This has been quite the deep dive into the backstory. I would apologize for how long it has become but had I not given you the backstory, the impact of the significance of what I'm about to tell you would probably be exponentially less.

This chapter is potentially the most important chapter of this book—if not, and I don't say this lightly—the most important chapter of any book of the 31 I have written so far.

I'm a visual person. At this moment, I don't see my mom and mother-in-law at the roulette table. I see you. You're possibly a part of one of these scenes:

1. You're on the edge of your seat, waiting (less and less) patiently for me to get to this way-overhyped roulette story. But you're into it, it's working for you and you see the possibilities and are interested for your own self and potential.
2. You're intrigued, prepared, probably a little (or a lot) skeptical, but ready to be open to what's ahead.
3. You have returned this book to the bookstore or have tossed it in flaming oil barrel of garbage in your backyard as you curse the last 17 minutes it had taken you to get this far.

I'm laughing out loud as I type this because, seven years ago, I would have been number three. A few short years ago, I would have been number two. Now I'm squarely in number one.

I hope you're in one or two. Well, if you were number three, you're no longer reading anymore anyway.

I feel I must interject a note about humor and humility here.

I laugh quite a bit. I even laugh in my meditations. My mom was funny. Not stand-up-comedian material, but silly and fun and sometimes funny. She could certainly laugh at herself not only with herself. This is key. If we can't laugh at ourselves, we're going to have a much harder time laughing at all.

These are crucial elements for the story:

1. I can laugh **with** myself
2. I can laugh **at** myself

It may seem odd to you that I'm offering up all of this backstory and apologies and explanation and maybe even excuses about why I'm writing this chapter.

The thing is, not only would I have not much believed anything in this chapter some years ago, had I believed it in the slightest, I wouldn't have admitted it to myself much less publicly.

Here I am, only a few short years later, and not only am I about to admit that I have regular conversations with my deceased parents but I'm writing about it publicly.

I see it as a bold leap of daring that can show you I have little fear of what you think and less and less fear of—remember our harshest critic?—what I think.

I feel I have set the scene well enough by now. If it is not yet enough for you or it's not quite clear, find me, contact me, and let me know how I can explain it more. I love, love, love talking about this especially with those of us ready and open for it.

Finally.

Here we go.

Roulette

It was early in the morning just a few days before my mother-in-law passed away in May of 2021.

Although I mentioned above that I'm more of an active meditator than a passive one, one of the best techniques I've learned along the way is to step into the void (the darkness, the space, the universe, whatever you want to call it) and be open to whatever is on the menu for the day.

It's much like a non-chain restaurant where they have a weekly special. If it's what fresh and what they're cooking that week, it's probably the best bet. Just like you shouldn't order a burger at the Chinese restaurant. Let them choose for you. *Then* you can be active.

The scene opens up (yes, it's very much like theater for me) and my mom is sitting at the roulette table.

The significance of this is that my mom and dad, Miss Summa Cum Laundry and Mr. Masters Degree in Mathematics, thought (well, they know) that roulette is pure chance. (Pro Gambling/Math Tip: it is.) They much preferred blackjack where there was some skill involved and percentages and projections and experience.

Yet roulette was just pure chance.

However, my mother-in-law, Bep, loved roulette.

When my wife and I were married in Lake Tahoe, Nevada, we later brought my Dutch mother-in-law to the glory and glamor of Reno.

She was more accustomed to Monte Carlo and it was going to take a little getting used to with the cheese-o-rama factor of penny slots, free watered-down cocktails, and chain-smoking local diehards.

Although, it didn't take *that* long.

I can still see my parents and my mother-in-law at the roulette table all of those years ago, piña colada in hand, and laughing and *strategizing* (apologies to the math geeks reading this...) about what numbers to pick next.

My mother-in-law doesn't speak too much English and my parents had been brushing up on their Dutch but had capped out somewhere along the lines of "Mooi!" (Beautiful) and "Gezellig!" (Cozy) and for the bonus points, "Allemachtig Prachtig" (almightily gorgeous), which you can say more easily if you have a sore throat— or want one.

Cocktails and roulette tends to bond strangers—even across language barriers. As does laughing and deep and love among family.

So the idea that my mom was at the roulette table in my meditation a few days before the passing of my mother-in-law was telling.

Although it was busy and noisy, there was a seat open next to my mom and she looked past me, to my right, and patted the stool next to her as if to say, this seat is available.

Behind me and to my right, somewhat offstage (remember, I see this often like a stage play), is Bep. She's peeking her head through a curtain and won't come further.

She looks around a bit but is hesitant.

My mom says something along the lines of, "I'm here for you. This seat is reserved for you. I'm always here for you. Take your time. But also, I have to say that I can't wait for you to get here—we're going to have so much fun."

Bep smiled nervously, looked around a bit more, and then went back behind the curtain and that was the end of my meditation.

Writing out how this transpired takes me much longer than to experience them during my meditations. Much like dreams, lots can happen and, just like a movie or a play, it takes much longer to explain or describe what happened.

The day after Bep passed away, the scene reappeared for me. This time, she came through the curtain and went to sit next to my mom. Bep was still rather hesitant and cautious as she didn't quite know where she was or why. But mom, caring and considerate as ever, took it slow and steady.

They played roulette a while (with number 17 being the obvious first choice as it's Bep's birthday and my wedding anniversary with her daughter). They had piña coladas. They laughed.

Bep wasn't yet completely comfortable and mom recognized it.

I don't always get words as spoken language as much as a knowing as to what they're saying. Maybe it's a bit like subtitles at the opera.

Bep asked my mom if this was it, if this was what it was all about. Not wanting to seem ungrateful, she thought it was fun and they were having a good time, but Bep stood up and said, "I have things I want to do."

My mom knew exactly what her friend wanted to do, stood up with her, put one last bet on 17, and said, "Let's get to it."

"Who do you want to help first?" my mom asked.

Bep seemed a little taken aback that my mom knew what she was thinking. The awkwardness lasted only seconds as the whole scene was still so new and full of surprises and that must have been one of the surprises that Dede knew her thoughts.

The casino scene quickly dissolved and the two of them were walking side by side in the desert away from where I could see them.

They were talking about who they were going to help and the order in which they were going to do it. My mom was explaining how it worked.

My mom was giddy like a schoolgirl to have her friend at her side, one with whom she shared her giving, loving, energy of helping others.

> *I can't see the screen as I type this as my eyes are full of tears. I'll have to come back and check for spelling mistakes.*

As much as I wanted to hear more, experience more, they walked away from where I could see and I soon could no longer hear them as they walked.

Their body language showed a friendship, a kinship, a family bond of people who were on a mission together that they both wanted to, couldn't wait to get started with.

As they left my scene, I noticed something I wish I could have a photo of as I would frame it and put it on my wall.

These two women, these two angels of the power of the universe, walking in the desert, laughing together as they set out, were holding hands.

Holding hands as they bonded together their power of giving, their talents of listening, their sharing of experience, and most of all, their unending, bottomless well of the deepest and sweetest love.

Repossible

- **Possible:** hope

- **Impossible:** deny
- **Repossible:** love

21

VIGNETTES

SOME THINGS ABOUT FAMILY ARE NEVER KNOWN

"Definition of Vignette. Vignette is a small impressionistic scene, an illustration, a descriptive passage, a short essay, a fiction or nonfiction work focusing on one particular moment; or giving an impression about an idea, character, setting, mood, aspect, or object. Vignette is neither a plot nor a full narrative description."

— Mom

As you'll read about below, I *convinced* (OK, fine, *nagged*) my mom to write down some stories from her life—especially the ones we kids might not have known about.

She called them vignettes and she got started on them and when we talked on the phone, I would ask her (nicely!) how it was going.

She said the cancer slowed down her creativity and mental acuity so it was harder in the end but she did manage to get some done.

Here is her introduction to them. I'll come back afterwards and *nag* you, I mean, *convince* you to create your own vignettes for your kids (and grandkids).

So what are these "vignettes" about? Why am I writing them?

Well, to be honest, my son, your father and uncle, convinced me (nagged me) into it. But he was right. Some things about family are never known. Some ideas are never expressed. Maybe you would like to know where you came from, who your ancestors were, what they did right and what didn't turn out so well.

And, truth be told, here is my chance to talk to you about a lot of subjects. I have no idea how this is going to turn out or what I am going to say. Just remember, I love you so much that I can't even type that without crying.

A colleague of Brad's suggested it would be good to focus on a photograph that evokes a memory. Sometimes I am sure I will do that backwards: I have something I want to say and remember an old or a recent picture that helps to set the mood or tell the story.

So, dear grandchildren, I plan to have fun doing this. But I won't stick to the happy "Brady Bunch" memories that other people perceive I have experienced. I'll try to be honest. Sometimes that it really hard. I've been called "The Queen of Denial" which is often not far from the truth.

I hope these vignettes will give you a glimpse inside yourself to understand who you are.

— Mom/Grandma/Dede

I'm going to copy and paste this one paragraph again:

> *"And, truth be told, here is my chance to talk to you about a*
> *lot of subjects. I have no idea how this is going to turn*
> *out or what I am going to say. Just remember, I love*
> *you so much that I can't even type that without crying."*

Are you familiar with the quote, usually attributed to Winston Churchill that he apologized for writing a long speech because he didn't have time to write a short one?

Over my writing career, I'm becoming more and more of a fan of shorter works. Sure, if it's a novel and there's backstory and scene-building, great, fine, I get it.

You may have noticed the book you have in your hands is not a biography. I don't start out with "Diane Mall Charbonneau was born on December 8 ... " and I don't finish up with, " ... and she passed away on ... " Nope. Not going there. Who would want to read that anyway? I'm her son and even I wouldn't want to read it.

Short, scenes, stories. Vignettes.

Let's take a look at this one paragraph of mom's that encapsulates so much in three sentences.

"Truth be told"

I like to see it like this: she wanted to write these stories, to share them with us, so she was secretly grateful that I nagged (and convinced) her to write them.

"Here is my chance"

As an author, I hear this from most soon-to-be authors, "I just want to tell my story. I want to be heard."

Mom writes that this is her chance, her opportunity to tell her story. What if your mom or dad (or aunt, uncle, grandparent, neighbor) was simply never asked to tell their story? Maybe they wanted to tell it but they never "got the chance" because no one ever asked them to tell it?

What if you, yes, you, dear reader, because the person who asked someone to tell their story? What if you took it a step further and enabled them to tell it? Maybe you just listened, sat with them for a short time and closed your mouth, maybe even closed your eyes, opened your ears and gave them the chance to tell their story?

What might that bring? What joy, pleasure, letting go and who-knows-what-other emotion might that bring about in them?

What might it bring about in *you*?

"To talk to you about a lot of subjects"

She was ready to let loose with all kinds of stories. She wanted to tell us kids.

At my dad's memorial service, mom had Liam (my oldest son, then 11-years-old) read a cowboy poem ("Do It Now" by Berton Braley). The end of the poem reads:

> *"If he earns your praise – bestow it,*
> *if you like him let him know it,*
> *Let the words of true encouragement be said;*
> *Do not wait till life is over*
> *and he's underneath the clover,*
> *For he cannot read his tombstone when he's dead."*

Don't regret the stories they didn't tell but cherish those they did.

"I have no idea how this is going to turn out or what I am going to say."

I run a program called "How to Write Your Worst Book Ever." I wish mom had been around for it. It's about breaking through, getting unstuck, and first writing a terrible book (or doing something wrong or making mistakes) and then later doing whatever it is you were so sure was so important.

She just started, she didn't know how it was going to turn out but she got started.

May I interject here to you, dear reader, how important this is for those of you who are along a bit further in years and haven't told your stories or written them down or recorded them or even told your kids (or friends or family).

If not now, then when? Or as the cowboy poet says, do it now.

She had no idea how it was going to turn out, if was going to be "any good" or not but she started. Do you want to ask me how grateful I am that she started and didn't get hung up on perfection, procrastination, and even probabilities?

> *"If you like him, if you love him, tell him now."*

Now.

> *"Don't withhold your approbation*
> *till the parson makes oration"*

How long should you wait?

> *"Do not wait till life is over*
> *and he's underneath the clover,*
> *For he cannot read his tombstone when he's dead."*

"Just remember, I love you so much that I can't even type that without crying."

Kids won't quite understand the love a parent has for a child until they have their own. Although it might not always even have to be a child, it could be a niece, a grandson, or a neighbor.

> *"I love you so much that I can't even type that without*
> *crying."*

How much?
She can't even type.
Is she thinking this and we'll never know about it?
No.
She's typing it.
She's logging it in the records for us to read, for now, forever.
But she's got to write it down, get it out, tell her story, tell us, tell you.
She also has to do it before ... *the parson makes oration.*

Repossible

- **Possible:** think about your stories
- **Impossible:** think about your stories (and let others read your mind)
- **Repossible:** share your stories

I'll find the full poem and put it up at ga.repossible.com.

AFTERWORD

"It is better to create than to learn! Creating is the essence of life."

— Julius Caesar

My intention with this book was rather simple:

1. Share some thoughts about mom
2. Share some stories from friends and family
3. Maybe inspire a reader or two to teach others, to give, to love more

The whole idea came about after I recorded that video the day before she passed and then a friend "pushed" me to write about it a few months later.

Because I'm a stickler for deadlines and when I say I'm going to do something, I do the thing, but I wasn't quite sure what the book was going to be, who it was for, or, in a weird way, why I was writing it.

I just knew I had to do it.

Now, having written it and having worked on it over the past months, having gathered stories from friends and family, and having received notes along the lines of "it's so great you're doing this" and hints from people who whispered "Gee, I wish my kids did this for me." Or even from not-yet-all-that-old folks who said, me included, something along the lines of, "Gee, I hope my kids might do even a fraction of something like this for me later."

But, true to mom's vision, she wasn't doing it for the praise, the thanks, or the fame.

She was going it because it was who she was: a giving, caring, teacher at heart.

For her, teaching others was her secret sauce, her super power. She had knowledge she could share, experience she could relate, and the voice and daring to offer it—whether those 7th-grade students wanted it or not.

Speaking of 7th-grade students who didn't want to be there, I have a book coming out soon called "You Don't Have To" although the original title was "You Don't Have To Write a Book."

Yep, those 7th graders *had to* be in school. But *you* don't have to read this book, you certainly don't have to be all the way back here in the afterword. I mean, seriously, who reads the afterword?

Well, clearly, you do.

So for those of you who are way back here, I have an idea, a proposition, a challenge.

I only thought of this thanks to one of my author students in my latest group of my "How to Write Your Worst Book Ever" program together with writing this book you have in your hands right now.

As I wrote this book, it became clear to me based on feedback from you that some of you might like to do something similar. Either writing a book with your own stories or writing a book of someone else's stories.

But then there are those pesky questions:

1. How do I get started?
2. What do I actually write about? How to structure it?
3. What if I hate writing?

4. What if I like the idea but think I'm a terrible writer, I can't spell, and/or my grammar is horrible?
5. What if I think it has to be a 749-page saga with every detail of mom's/dad's/my life that I'll never finish?
6. What about the idea that no one on the planet would care to read it?
7. But what about the idea that I'd really like to do this but am hesitant about doing it alone, don't know when or where or how to start but maybe if someone showed me the ropes and gave me some step-by-step walkthroughs of how to piece it together then maybe I could do this, right?

One thing mom was really good at was explaining things that were easy to her yet difficult to others. I like to think I inherited a bit of that from her.

You have my 31st book in your hands. I think I now have more books than socks (or at least matching socks without holes in them...).

I'm becoming more and more of an advocate for books that:

1. Are short
2. Have a simple or even single idea
3. Don't have extraneous mountains of malarkey
4. Are fun for the author to read
5. Are fun for the reader to read (see #4: if you have #4, you get #5 usually as a bonus)
6. Don't wait for perfection
7. Beat procrastination on a regular basis
8. Need to be told
9. Want to be shared
10. Get done

As I write this, I don't have such a program on offer but I'm thinking about it and the more I think about it, the better and better it sounds.

Because I have to get this book published, I'm going to give you a link here where can go find out more about this idea and let me know if you'd be interested in some sort of program (or workshop or course or challenge) where we'd get short vignettes done either about our own lives to share with our kids or for someone else like a parent.

I like the word *trigger*. I also like being a trigger or a catalyst. Who knows, it took me recording a video about mom the day before she passed and then a friend saying I should write a book about it for it to materialize for me.

Maybe for you it's this book and then this afterword where it clicks, it triggers the idea in you for you to do something similar.

Head over to ga.repossible.com where you'll get access to the Bonus Content for this book and we can there build on the discussion about you writing your own book.

If you want to know what I *really* think about "creating" versus "consuming," have a look at one my favorite books I wrote, Create. To put it simply, creating is one of the secrets to living a life of meaning and purpose and joy.

Repossible

- **Possible:** consume
- **Impossible:** get from consuming what you get from creating
- **Repossible:** create

ACKNOWLEDGMENTS

This entire book has pretty much been an acknowledgment to my mom but hey, for one last hurrah, I want to thank my mom and dad.

In the afterword I mentioned triggers and how this book came because I did a video about mom and then a friend of mine, Jeroen, really pressed me to write about it.

Sure, lots of people say to lots of other people, "Hey, you should write a book about that!" But it's almost like asking, "How are you?" when you don't really want to know.

But this one was genuine. He really meant it—and I felt it.

I thank the triggers that brought this book into its creation.

Who will you thank when you have your book done?

ABOUT THE AUTHOR

The first person to buy my books was always my mom. She's not going to get this one.

That makes me sad.

So I could mope around the house and feel sorry for myself or I could harness her energy, her power, and her love and help spread it further.

I have a book called "Decide." The subtitle for that book is one of my favorites, "There's usually a choice. It's usually yours."

We don't have a choice about our past. It's done. It's over.

We can't change the future right now.

We can change the present (which will alter our future).

So if I have a choice to mope around the house in sorrow or allow myself to try to fill the shoes of my mom and scatter her powers to those who might benefit from it, which sounds like more fun? Which one is more empowering both for me and those who receive her love?

I now don't have any parents left. My kids don't have any grandparents left. Who is going to tell the stories?

Who will tell your stories?

There's a fine line between hearing and listening. Remember the train in Europe? The *this-is-so-boring* stories about the price of grain in Kansas? Or was it Oklahoma?

My sister and I might have not have been *listening*, in fact, we might have been proactively *not listening*, but we were *hearing*.

The sounds, the voices, the stories, seeped into our brains, lodged into our memories, and, whether we wanted them there or not, they stayed there.

The stories don't have to be told. The parents don't have to tell them and the kids don't have to listen. Remember my upcoming book? *You Don't Have To*.

No, you don't have to. We have a choice.

That choice is yours.

I choose to write down the stories.

I hope this book inspires you to write down yours—or those of others you love.

I currently live in a little town outside of Utrecht in The Netherlands with my wife Saskia, famous two young boys of "The Adventures of Li & Lu" fame, and our at-least-as-famous dog Pepper.

This is my thirty-first book.

It is far, far, far, like oh-so-far from my last.

Find, ask, discuss, play, dare, and surrender at:
bradleycharbonneau.com

facebook.com/bradley.charbonneau.author

twitter.com/brathocha

instagram.com/brathocha

amazon.com/author/bradleycharbonneau

bookbub.com/profile/bradley-charbonneau

goodreads.com/bradleycharbonneau

linkedin.com/in/likoma

patreon.com/repossible

pinterest.com/likoma

ALSO BY BRADLEY CHARBONNEAU

Most of my books are also available as audiobooks (which I giddily narrate). Search for my name at your favorite audiobook distributor, slip on your headphones, and let me take you away.

Repossible

Who Will You Be Next?

1. Repossible
2. Every Single Day (+ Playbook)
3. Ask
4. Dare
5. Create (also available: Box Set #1)
6. Decide
7. Meditate
8. Spark (also available: Box Set #2)
9. Surrender
10. Play
11. Celebrate (also available: Box Set #3 and Box Set Complete)
12. Evaluate (2022)
13. Elevate (2022)
14. Give (2022)

Authorpreneur

Beyond the Book

1. You Don't Have To
2. How to Write Your Worst Book Ever

3. The One-Word-Long Book that Will Probably Change
   Your Life
4. Write
5. Publish
6. Market
7. Boost Your Brand with a Book
8. MailerLite for Authors
9. Audio for Authors
10. Chapter Won

Charlie Holiday

The Chance is Yours

1. Now Is Your Chance
2. Second Chance
3. Chance of a Lifetime (also available: Box Set)

Short Trips

Just Put on the Shoes

1. Secret Bus to Paradise
2. Where I (Already) Am
3. Pass the Sour Cream
4. A Trip to Hel
5. Goddamn Attitude
6. Drive-By Dropping

Li & Lu

Bring Adventure Home

1. The Secret of Kite Hill
2. The Secret of Markree Castle

3. The Key to Markree Castle
4. The Gift of Markree Castle
5. Driehoek (also available: Box Set)

Really Old ...

urban travel guide SAN FRANCISCO

www.ingramcontent.com/pod-product-compliance
Lightning Source LLC
Chambersburg PA
CBHW020739160726

47993CB00006B/2520